CW01369670

Future Leader
7 Prophetic Declarations for
Shaping Your Child's Identity
(For Girls)

Copyright © 2022 by Gbenga Ogunjimi

All rights reserved. No part of this publication may be reproduced, stored in a retrieval system, or transmitted in any form or by any means, electronic, mechanical, photocopying, recording, scanning, or otherwise, without the prior written permission of the author except for the use of quotations in a book review.

Book illustration by TulipStudio
Edited by Erika Ogunjimi

ISBN: 978-1-7323911-2-3

Dedication

To our first child, Obatide Josiah Ogunjimi, your mom and I are eternally thankful that God chose us to be your parents and to purposefully participate in your journey as a Future Leader.

- Love Daddy

Train up a child in the way he should go: and when he is old,
he will not depart from it.
Proverbs 22:6 (KJV)

Introduction

I wrote the Future Leader book to answer a simple question - How are thought leaders raised or how do they come about?

When I look at leaders that have changed the world, have great names, and those that are celebrated in history, one thing is very clear about them: their parents were not accidental about their greatness. They were very intentional from day one and, in most cases, way before the children came along the parents were visionary in their approach. They had a clear picture of the type of person they wanted to bring into the world. And while there may be several tools out there for how you can raise and foster greatness in your child, I wrote this prayer book from a Christian perspective, particularly using words of affirmation and prophetic declarations.

I also realize that there is an existing format and practice where parents form a bond with their children through bedtime stories. While we know that bedtime stories may not fully be comprehended by children at an early age, the process still forms an emotional bond between a parent and a child. But if that is all bedtime stories are used for, I feel that is a missed opportunity.

While this is not a typical "story book", Future Leader bridges that gap. Furthermore, from a Christian standpoint, we can use these prophetic declarations to not only foster an emotional bond but also to speak into the destiny of our children.

We know this to be true because Bible scriptures are full of examples of thought leaders coming into greatness through prophetic declaration. We saw it happen in the book of Jeremiah when God spoke to Jeremiah and said, "Before I formed you in your mother's womb, I've ordained you as a prophet to the nations." Through the act of prophetic declarations, over time we saw that greatness materialize in Jeremiah. This example is particularly telling of how God did not give or defer that responsibility to the child to figure out on his own. Instead he declared it over his life. We are using this same format to get the Future Leader message across. I believe this prophetic leadership role is a responsibility every parent should take in forming their child's identity.

To Parents - How to Use This Book

1. **Daily Reading** - Use this as an accompaniment to your daily spiritual practices such as bible reading, prayer, or meditation. Read this to your children during early ages, yes - even in the womb and include it as an option for bedtime reading. As they begin to expand their vocabulary, have them read it aloud to you replacing the "You" with "I"; and as they move into young adulthood, have them include it as a part of their own personal reading.

2. **Journaling** - Journal your experience and thoughts that come as a result of this book. How does it translate to you? Pay close attention to images that appear and the new set of vocabulary that this book inspires in you or your child. Also use journaling to track your language. If needed, explore ways to change your or your child's language to make sure it is consistent with speaking leadership over your child's life.

3. **Activities** - Future Leader is a conversation starter around the topics of purpose, leadership, and identity. Discuss with your children what it means to be one of the 7 leadership identities explored in this book. Have your children describe what the concepts mean to them in their own words. Make it fun for your children and create activities surrounding the Future Leader themes.

4. Special Occasions - Use this book to pray over your children at special events such as baby showers, baby dedications, and naming ceremonies. Use it at the start of birthdays, each new year, and new journeys such as the first day of school, starting new jobs, and going off to college.

Finally, let this content challenge you (the parent and child) to imagine what being a future leader means.

Now let's get started.

The Future Leader Prayer

In the name of Jesus Christ, I make these declarations over you today.

I declare concerning you, _____, that you are:

- A Woman of God,
- A Wealth Creator,
- A Changemaker,
- A Thought Leader,
- A History Maker,
- A Woman of Integrity, and
- A Global Blessing.

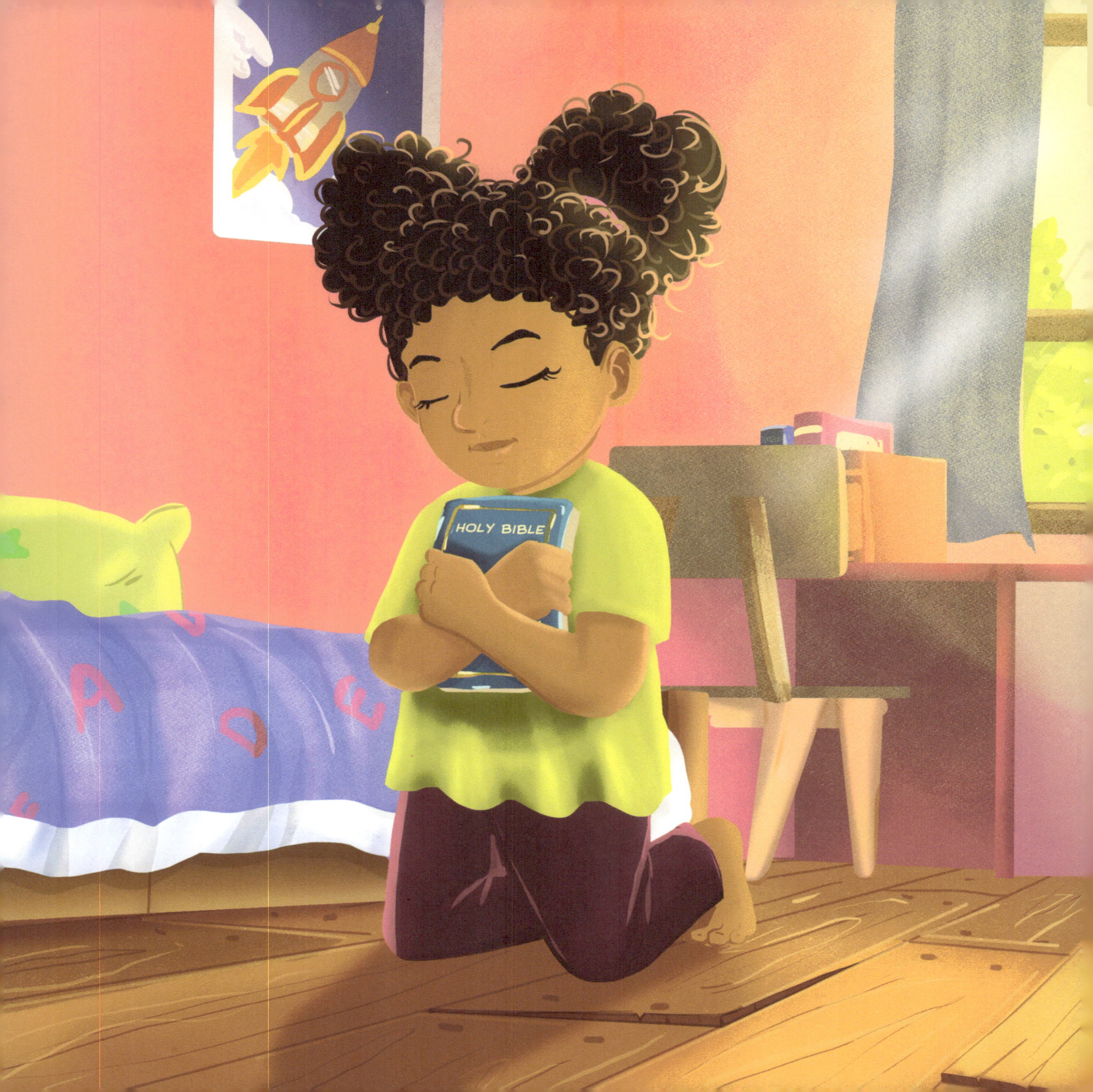
HOLY BIBLE

YOU ARE A WOMAN OF GOD

*For we are God's masterpiece. He has created us anew in Christ Jesus,
so we can do the good things he planned for us long ago.*
Ephesians 2:10 NLT

You are a living testimony of the power of God. You are a walking miracle and a gift of God to the world. God has placed a powerful call over your life to change the world. You are the closest to God many will see in their lifetime. There will never come a time that you will struggle with your spiritual, gender, professional or cultural identity.

"Your identity is rock solid in Jesus Christ."

You will not struggle to find your husband, power circle, true friends, teachers, advisors, mentors, coaches, or spiritual parents. You are a woman of prayer. You have a direct communication channel to the throne room of God. When you pray angels will be summoned and God shall respond affirmatively and rapidly to your prayers. Your words are borderless, powerful, and prophetic. God has given you the keys to his kingdom. Therefore you have a kingdom paradigm and an excellent spirit. You are God's representative on earth. You are God's answer to the problems of the world.

"The anointing of God is in you."

The Holy Spirit of God is in you and the angels of God watch over you. God is always working in you both to will and to do of his good purposes. Therefore you are a vessel of honor and co-creator with God. God has given you the spirit of power, love and sound judgement. You have God consciousness and sensitivity to the Holy Spirit. The fruit of the Spirit which is love, joy, peace, patience, kindness, goodness, faithfulness, gentleness and self-control are evident in your life and form your personality, temperament and personal brand. You will not grieve the Holy Spirit a day in your life. Jesus Christ will forever be your Lord and Savior. You are a woman of God.

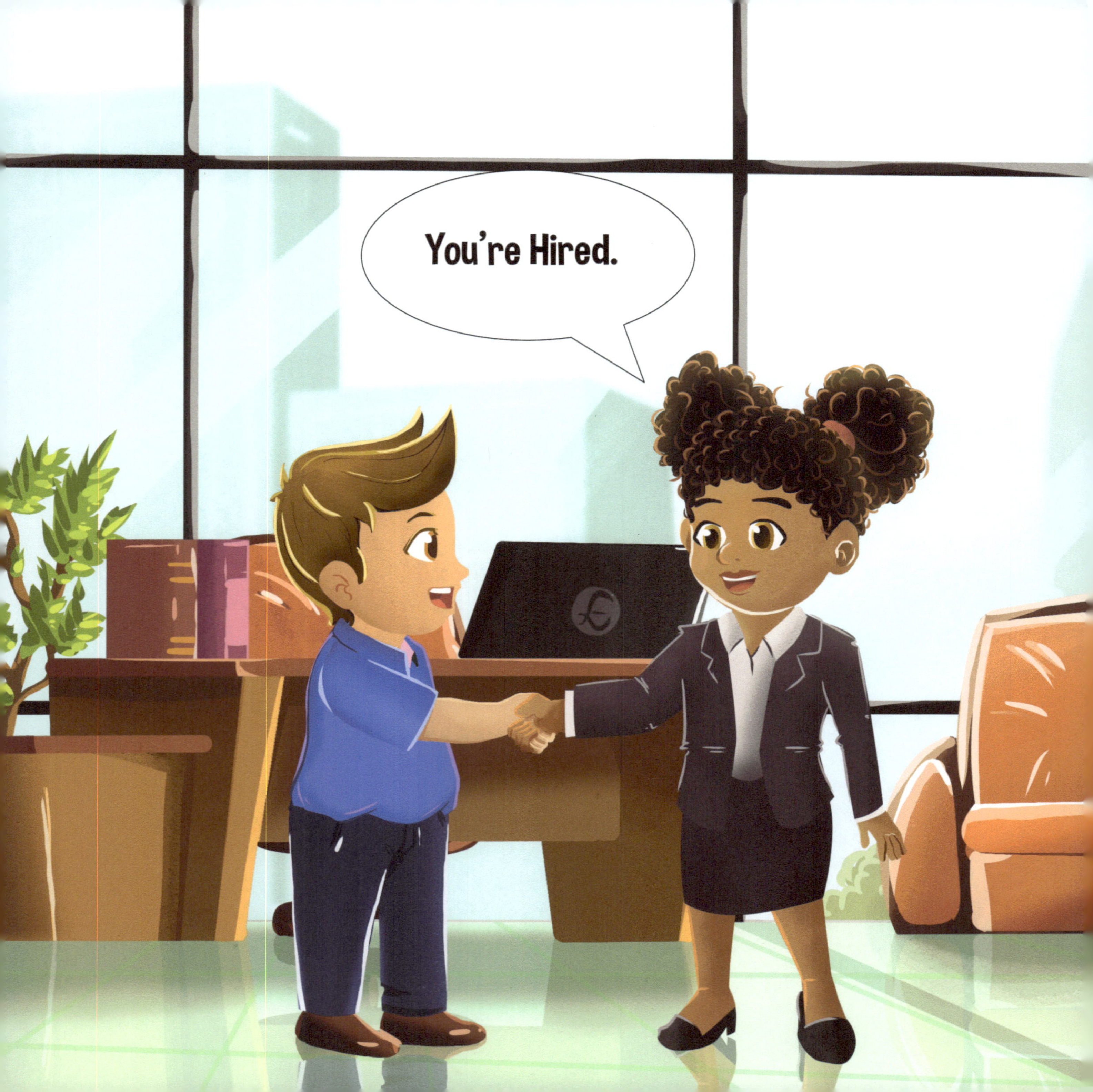
You're Hired.

YOU ARE A WEALTH CREATOR

*And the man became great and gained more and more
until he became very wealthy and extremely distinguished.*
Genesis 26:13 AMP

You are a mighty woman of wealth. God has given you the power to create wealth. You have come into great wealth and that wealth shall extend to future generations. You create wealth and do not work for money. It is your money that works for you. Because it has been written concerning you that you will live all your days in prosperity and your years in pleasures, you will never be broke a day in your life. You are financially literate and business savvy. You think outside of the box. You have an abundance mentality.

"You speak and understand the language of wealth."

There are no limits, lack or scarcity in your consciousness. Money comes to you effortlessly and money in your hands is a force for good. You shall owe no man nothing. According to the word of the Lord, for the **LORD** your God will bless you as he has promised, and you will lend to many nations but will borrow from none. You will rule over many nations but none will rule over you. You will leave an inheritance for your children's children. Your children shall arise and call you a blessed mother. Your husband also will honor you and call you blessed as well. You are planted in the house of the **LORD**.

"Wealth and riches shall be in your house."

You will flourish in the courts of our God. You will thrive and prosper even in old age. You will flourish and stay green. You shall declare that the **LORD** is upright and faithful to His promises towards you. You shall declare, God is my rock, and there is no unrighteousness in Him. You are a wealth creator.

YOUR VOTE COUNTS

YOU ARE A CHANGEMAKER

Let your light so shine before men, that they may see your good works,
and glorify your Father which is in heaven.
Matthew 5:16 KJV

You come from a lineage of changemakers, changemaking is in your DNA. You are the change the world is seeking and has been praying for. And because of your ideas, innovations, inventions, and vision, the world is a better and more prosperous place. You do not conform to this world or its cultures, instead, God has placed you here as a catalyst for change. When Nelson Mandela was born, freedom came to the people of South Africa. When Mahatma Gandhi and Mother Teresa were born, freedom came to the people of India. When Harriet Tubman was born, freedom came to African Americans in America. Because you have come to the world, freedom has come to your family, community, country, and the nations of the world.

"You are here to change the world."

Therefore arise and take your place among the world-changers and changemakers. You do not idly wait for change to happen, instead, you make change happen. You are a critical and strategic thinker. You have the mind of Christ, your thoughts are original and defies the status quo. Your thoughts are honest, just, pure, lovely, virtuous, praiseworthy and of good report.

"You can do all things through Christ who strengthens you."

You are a community leader, a bridge-builder, a nation builder and a global shaper. According to the word of the Lord, you shall rebuild the old waste places; you shall raise up the foundations of many generations. You'll be known as one of those who can fix anything, restore old ruins, rebuild and renovate, and make broken communities livable again. You are a changemaker.

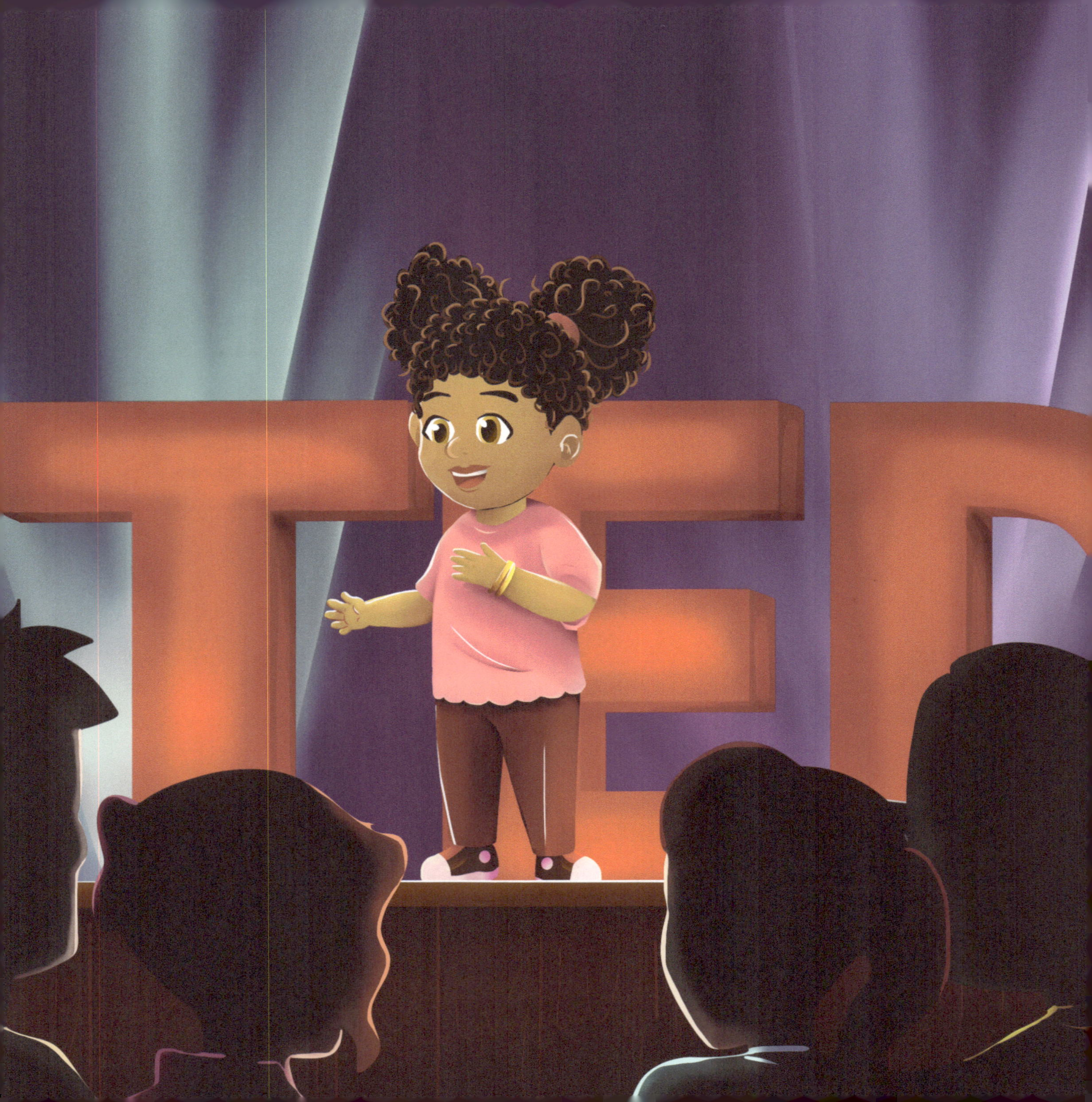

YOU ARE A THOUGHT LEADER

*The LORD your God will elevate you above all the nations of the earth.
Deuteronomy 28:1 NET Bible*

You are a born leader and a woman of purpose. God has assigned and uniquely wired you to prosper and dominate your industry. You are a leading voice and authority of this industry. You are the thought leader of your field. You are a trailblazer, trendsetter, pathfinder, and visionary leader. You are a builder of people. You have a coat of many colors; this means you have a borderless voice and multicultural influence.

"You know who you are."

May you never see yourself as marginalized, disadvantaged, oppressed, disenfranchised or subdued. May you never become a victim of identity theft, identity crisis, systemic oppression, racial prejudice, character assasination or cultural indoctrination. You've been pre-approved, justified and called by God. There is therefore now no condemnation concerning you because you belong to Christ Jesus. You have power with God and with men and women. You have favor with God and with men and women. This is the word of the Lord concerning you, the LORD your God will set you high above all the nations of the world. God declares concerning you today.

"All you have to do is ask, and I will give you the nations as your inheritance and the whole earth as your possession."

And as you go from one nation to another, God has authorized no man to do you harm. Therefore you shall never fear what any man or woman can do to you. God has permitted no one to abuse or oppress you. He has explicitly instructed kings and governments to keep their hands off you, saying; touch not my anointed, and do my prophets no harm. You are a thought leader.

M. TERESA &
N. MANDELA &
M. GANDHI &
H. TUBMAN

YOU ARE A HISTORY MAKER

Although Abel is long dead, he still speaks to us by his example of faith.
Hebrews 11:4 NLT

You walk by faith and not by sight. You are a woman of great and everlasting faith. Although you have come to this world as an individual, when it is your time to leave, you are going to leave here as an institution. Generations yet to be born will read about your life story and celebrate your life's work. Your name will not fade away with the passing of time but instead, you will make history. Your contributions and legacy shall outlive you. Your name is etched in the pages of history as a great name. Institutions, foundations and endowments shall be in your name.

"You have a good and honorable name."

Parents around the world shall name their children after you. Streets, boulevards, avenues, and highways shall be named in your honor. Books shall be written in celebration of your contributions to the world. History shall be kind to you. You have a powerful voice and your words have systemic and political ramifications.

"Nations shall recognize your voice, anointing and mantle."

According to the word of the Lord concerning you; The LORD shall make you the head, and not the tail; and you shall be above only, and you shall not be beneath. And because you are born of God, you overcome the world. You are blessed. Therefore be fruitful, and multiply, and replenish the earth, and subdue it: and have dominion. You are a history maker.

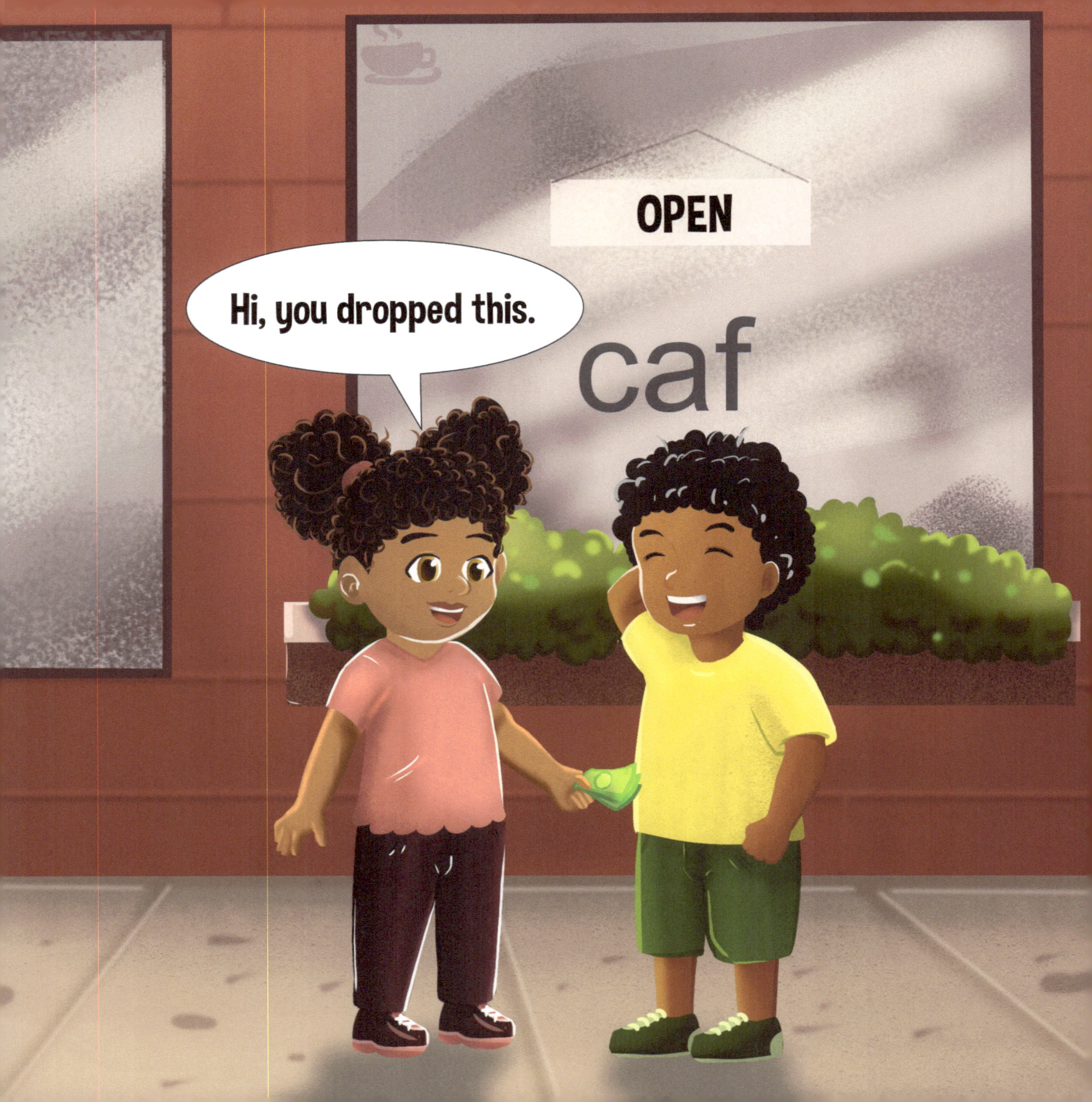
OPEN
Hi, you dropped this.
caf

YOU ARE A WOMAN OF INTEGRITY

You will walk in the way of good men [that is, those of personal integrity, moral courage and honorable character], And keep to the paths of the righteous.
Proverbs 2:20 AMP

You are the salt of the earth. What this means is that you are an ethical leader. You are a virtuous and righteous woman. There is no amount of pressure or money in this world that will make you compromise your integrity. You are generous, just, and fair in all your dealings. You are an advocate for the vulnerable, unrepresented and marginalized. You are a woman of substance, nobility, and wisdom. Your personal brand is associated with credibility, authority, and excellence. Your brand has global attention and recognition. You have a forgiving spirit. You will never harbor unforgiveness, envy, or malicious intention against anyone a day in your life. No one shall harbor the same concerning you, and if anyone does it will never materialize because no weapon formed against you shall prosper."

"Your integrity is not for sale."

God is in you. God is for you. The words of your mouth are honorable, powerful, and profitable. You will speak of excellent things; and the opening of your lips shall be the right things. For your mouth shall always speak truth. Your mouth shall bring forth wisdom and good news. Because iron sharpens iron; you walk in the companionship of the wise, the wealthy, the powerful, the visionary, and the God-fearing. There shall be no one in your circle or remotely close to you unauthorized by God.

"God is with you. You cannot fail."

Everyone in your life is there on a divine assignment. You shall honor all men. You are the body of Christ and your body is the temple of the living God. Therefore you live a life that is trauma-free, debt-free, drama-free, depression-free, scandal-free, addiction-free, and disease-free. You are a woman of integrity.

Let's Change the World!

YOU ARE A GLOBAL BLESSING

I will make you into a great nation, and I will bless you;
I will make your name great, and you will be a blessing.
Genesis 12:2 NIV

For as long as you are in the world, there is plenty of light. You are the light of the world. This means you are an innovator, and your creations will change the world. You have come to the world for such a time like this. Your community and country are blessed because you live in them. You walk in the path of wisdom and this path shines brighter and brighter on a daily basis.

"You are necessary and indispensable to this world."

Therefore arise and shine for the glory of God has come upon you. You are a woman of power, authority, and influence. You are a leader in your community and country. You are a global leader. You seek the peace and prosperity of your city and country. You are blessed, fruitful, and strong. You are a great nation.

"You will be the mother of many nations."

This is the covenant of God with you: For I have made you a mother of many nations. I will make you very fruitful; I will make nations of you, and kings will come from you. You are a leader to the world's leaders and a prophet to the nations. You are a global blessing.

I declare above all things you will prosper and be in good health even as your soul prospers. I declare that the eyes of your understanding be flooded with light by the Holy Spirit-to make you intelligent and discerning - and by knowing Him personally, you can see exactly and live out fully what it is He has called you to do. I pray that you live a purpose-driven and God-centered life.

And finally I declare, may the Lord your God bless you, and keep you. May he make his face shine upon you, and be gracious to you. May he multiply your peace and bless you with his favor.

May he bless you today as:

- A Woman of God,
- A Wealth Creator,
- A Changemaker,
- A Thought Leader,
- A History Maker,
- A Woman of Integrity, and
- A Global Blessing.

In Jesus' mighty name.
Amen.

Acknowledgements

I'd like to thank my wife and life partner, Erika Ogunjimi, for the opportunity to raise our son and future children as future leaders. I thank you for helping me to bring this book to life. Thank you for challenging me to create this resource for our child which has now become a resource that we are now sharing with the world.

I want to thank my parents, Tajudeen Ogunjimi and Omolara Amure, for role-modeling what it means to raise a future leader. You are the ones that instilled in me the discipline of prayer that has now become my life strategy and superpower. Thank you for giving me the greatest gift a parent can give his child, which is the knowledge of their true identity and heritage.

Thank you to my spiritual mentor, Dr. Cindy Trimm, for teaching me the identity-framing power of prayer, and how the simple act of elevating one's language can elevate one's leadership in the world.

Lastly, I am grateful to Mr. Richard Williams, for writing the book Black and White: The Way I See It. Thank you for being generous enough to share with the world your genius as a father raising women who have changed the culture, their industry, and the world.

About The Author
Gbenga Ogunjimi

Gbenga is a West African name that means "elevate" which has led him to his life's purpose of elevating leaders to overcome the gap of access holding them back from making imprints on the global stage. Gbenga is the Executive Producer of Good to Great Stories: A Small Business Documentary.

His premier book, Borderless Voice: The Power of Telling Your Story and Defining Your Identity, is a compilation of stories and strategies that shows readers how to harness the power of their story. Gbenga is happily married and currently resides in Washington DC with his family. For more information or to contact Gbenga Ogunjimi, visit www.gbenga.org.

Lightning Source UK Ltd.
Milton Keynes UK
UKHW050904130223
416655UK00017BA/113